Patterns

This math series is dedicated to Nick, Tony, Riley, and Hailey.

Published by The Child's World®
PO Box 326
Chanhassen, MN 55317-0326
800-599-READ
www.childsworld.com

Design and Production: The Creative Spark, San Juan Capistrano, CA

All photography © David M. Budd Photography except as follows:
© John Conrad/CORBIS: 6
© CORBIS: 7
© Keren Su/CORBIS: 9
© Michael and Patricia Fogden/CORBIS: 12

Library of Congress Cataloging-in-Publication Data
Pistoia, Sara.
   Patterns / by Sara Pistoia.
       p. cm. — (Mighty math series)
Includes index.
Summary: Easy-to-read text introduces the idea of patterns.
   ISBN 1-56766-117-3 (lib. bdg. : alk. paper)
  1. Pattern perception—Juvenile literature. [1. Pattern perception.]
I. Title. II. Series.
  BF294 .P57 2002
  510—dc21
                                        2002005341

Patterns

Sara Pistoia

We use patterns to recognize all kinds of things in our world. Colors or shapes used over and over form a pattern.

You can see patterns on wrapping paper. You can see patterns on leaves and flowers.

These patterns are on animal fur. Can you guess which animals they are?

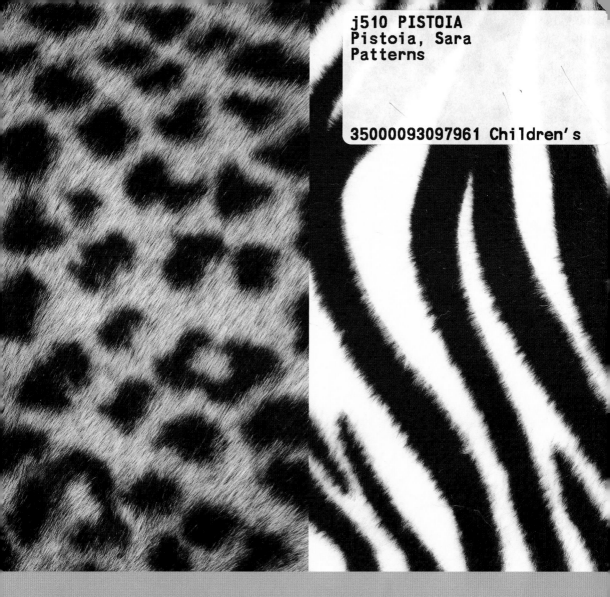

Hi! I'm Math Mutt! I'm here to help you learn about patterns. I can tell you about these animals, too. One is a leopard, and the other is a zebra.

The world would be different without patterns. Without stripes, this zebra would look like a plain horse!

Tigers and leopards are both wild cats. Is this a tiger or a leopard? You can tell by the stripes on its fur. Tigers have stripes. Leopards have spots.

Patterns can be made with shapes, sizes, colors, and positions.

Look at the animal on the next page. You know it's a panda because it looks like a panda. But what makes a panda look different from a grizzly bear?

Patterns help us sort and identify things in nature.

Pandas have white faces with black patches around their eyes. Where else do you see black patches? The panda's black and white coloring forms a pattern. That pattern makes it look different from any other animal.

Sometimes the parts of a pattern repeat themselves. When patterns repeat, it helps us think about what might come next.

These jelly beans form a pattern. The pattern uses colors and numbers. How can you tell what color comes next?

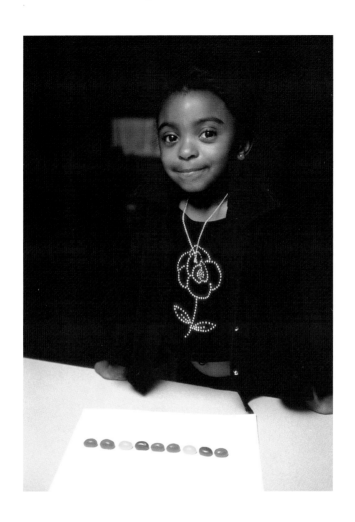

Think about the way the jelly beans are laid out. Red, red, yellow, green. Red, red, yellow, green. Now can you tell what color comes next?

Some patterns are simple,
like the stripes on this snake.
Do you see the pattern?
Red, black, yellow, black.
Red, black, yellow, black.

Some patterns aren't so simple. This wrapping paper has a pattern, but it keeps changing. Can you tell what might come next?

It's hard to know what would come next on this wrapping paper!

13

Knowing about patterns can help us in math class. You already know some patterns in math. When you count, you use a pattern:

0, 1, 2, 3, 4, 5, 6, 7, 8, 9 . . .

What comes next?

Did you say 10? You're right!

14

What happens when we reach 10? The pattern starts all over again!

But this time, we put a "1" in front of each number—10, 11,....

10, 11, 12, 13, 14, 15, 16, 17, 18, 19 . . .

Do you see the pattern?

Now try counting the peanuts on the next page. What happens when we reach 19? We start the pattern all over again at 20. Can you think of the last four numbers in this pattern?

Say, those peanuts look pretty tasty! May I have some when you're done counting?

The last four numbers are 27, 28, 29, and 30. Did the pattern change after 29? Yes! We used the number 3 and started the pattern all over again!

The days of the week form a pattern, too. Which day always comes after Sunday? Which day always comes after Wednesday?

Knowing the days of the week can help you solve this math problem. Let's say you leave home on Saturday to go to your grandma's house. It will take four days to get there. On what day will you arrive?

Saturday, Sunday, Monday, Tuesday—we'll be there Tuesday. I hope she'll make some cookies!

Look at this hundreds chart. Do you see patterns that can help you with math?

Count using all the numbers with yellow jelly beans. You are counting by fives. What about the last row? Would you know where to place the jelly beans to finish the pattern?

1	2	3	4	5	6	7	8	9	10
11	12	13	14	15	16	17	18	19	20
21	22	23	24	25	26	27	28	29	30
31	32	33	34	35	36	37	38	39	40
41	42	43	44	45	46	47	48	49	50
51	52	53	54	55	56	57	58	59	60
61	62	63	64	65	66	67	68	69	70
71	72	73	74	75	76	77	78	79	80
81	82	83	84	85	86	87	88	89	90
91	92	93	94	95	96	97	98	99	100

The yellow jelly bean numbers on this chart make a pattern that counts by fives. Let's study the pattern together. I'd say the numbers in the last row must be 95 and 100!

This musician thinks about patterns when he plays or writes music. Scientists think about finding patterns when they study plants. Artists think about patterns when they create a work of art.

Patterns of letters helped you learn to read. Discovering and using patterns is important in math, too.

If you start thinking about patterns, you can see them everywhere!

How have you used a pattern today?

Key Words

counting

fives

hundreds

identify

pattern

positions

recognize

repeat

solve

Index

About the Author

Sara Pistoia is a retired elementary teacher living in Southern California with her husband and a variety of pets. After 40 years of teaching, she now contributes to education by supervising and training student teachers at California State University at Fullerton. In authoring this series, she draws on the experience of many years of teaching first and second graders.